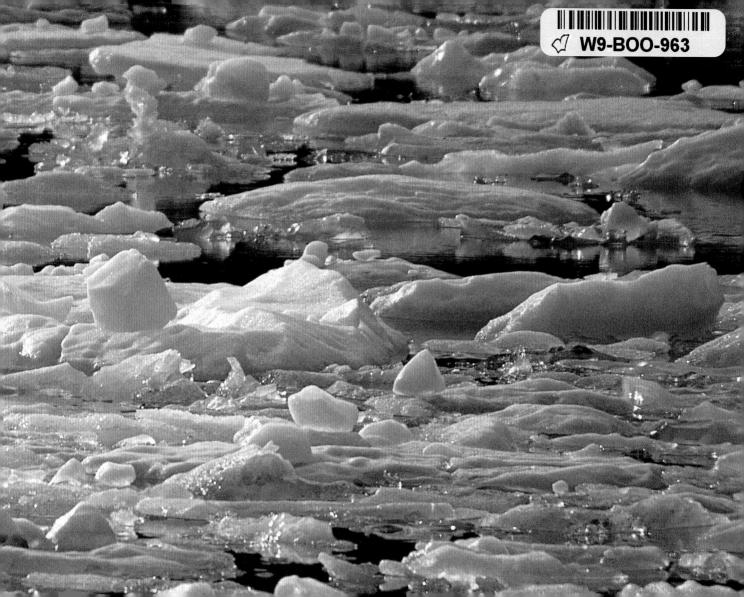

Alaska's
TRACY ARM & SAWYER GLACIERS

For Lowell and
Stephanie
Welcome to Alaska
May 21, 2008

Mark Kelley

Publisher and photographer: Mark Kelley
Writer: Nick Jans
Book and cover design: Laura Lucas
Printers: Samhwa Printing Company; Seoul, Korea

Single copies of *Alaska's Tracy Arm and Sawyer Glaciers* can be purchased for $14.95, plus $3.00 for shipping and handling. Retail discounts are available for stores.

Mark Kelley can be reached at P.O. Box 20470, Juneau, AK 99802;
by phone (toll free) at (888) 933-1993 or (907) 586-1993;
by fax at (907) 586-1201; or by e-mail at photos@markkelley.com
Web site: www.markkelley.com

Printed in Korea
First Edition March 2005
Second Printing January 2006
10 9 8 7 6 5 4 3 2

ISBN 0-9744053-3-7

COVER: Cruise ship travels toward South Sawyer Glacier in Tracy Arm.
ENDPAPERS: Icebergs at sunset jam waters in Tracy Arm.
HALF-TITLE PAGE: The day boat, *Adventure Bound*, passes in front of South Sawyer Glacier.
TITLE PAGE: The *Spirit of Columbia* approaches icebergs in Tracy Arm.
BACK COVER: Harbor seals haul out on icebergs for rest and protection from predators.

Our vessel glides inland, away from the sweep of ocean waves, threading between icebergs that shimmer blue and white. On either side of the narrowing passage, walls of sheer granite tower skyward, cut by waterfalls and cascades. Through binoculars, a distant speck above becomes a mountain goat; farther along, seals sunning on a raft of ice regard us with dark, liquid eyes. Carved glacial domes and ragged nunataks a mile above us reflect on the water's surface, and below our hull, the cold, green depths of the fjord whisper a tidal pulse old as time.

by NICK JANS

ABOVE: Harbor seal rests on iceberg.
RIGHT: Passengers on board a day tour boat cruise through icebergs on the way to Sawyer Glacier, often referred to as North Sawyer Glacier.

Mountain goat.

Tracy Arm: a rather ordinary name for an extraordinary place, arguably one of the most spectacular glacial fjords in both Alaska and the world. Glacier Bay National Park, roughly 125 miles to the northwest, is far better known, and Misty Fjords, near Ketchikan, is duly celebrated. But Tracy Arm, 32 miles long and averaging a mile wide, surrounded by steep mountain walls rising up to 7,000 feet from sea level, surrenders nothing in grandeur or vertical scale to any of these treasures. In fact, it gains its visual power from the fact that so much is crammed into such a compact space. It is, in its own right, the sort of place that's worth traveling halfway around the world to see, a landscape that reminds us, residents and travelers alike, of why we came to Alaska.

RIGHT: The Coast Mountains of Southeast Alaska are the backdrop for the Sawyer Glacier (North Sawyer Glacier). The Coast Mountains separate Alaska from Canada.

Two peaks rise more than 4,000 feet above the waters of Tracy Arm.

"A wild unfinished Yosemite"

Famed naturalist John Muir thought enough
of Tracy Arm to call it, after two visits in the
late 19th century, "a wild unfinished Yosemite,"
and to proclaim that "no ice work I have ever
seen surpasses this, either in the magnitude of
the features or effectiveness of composition."
Quite an accolade from a man who explored
some of the roughest and wildest terrain in the
Pacific Northwest, including Glacier Bay. Con-
sidering that the Grand Canyon, at its deepest
point, has 1,500 feet less vertical relief, it's
hardly an overstatement.

With a 7,000-foot peak rising in the background,
waterfalls cascade down thousands of feet of barren
rock walls recently revealed by the glacier's retreat.

SOUTHEAST ALASKA

Dayboat route from Juneau to Tracy Arm

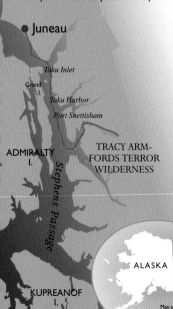

● **Juneau**

Taku Inlet

Grand
I.

Taku Harbor

Port Snettisham

**ADMIRALTY
I.**

**TRACY ARM-
FORDS TERROR
WILDERNESS**

Stephens Passage

**KUPREANOF
I.**

● **Petersburg**

ALASKA

Map area

Tracy Arm is the northernmost of three narrow fjords — Tracy, Endicott and Fords Terror — that together make up the Tracy Arm-Fords Terror Wilderness, about 45 miles southeast of Juneau. While relatively petite by Alaska standards, this preserve, overseen by the U.S. Forest Service, is nonetheless immense. Extending eastward to the Canadian border, it enfolds 653,179 acres of the ragged, soaring Coast Mountains, those three dramatic fjords and their meeting place at Holkham Bay, plus three tidewater glaciers (Sawyer, South Sawyer and Dawes) — not to mention a sizeable hunk of the sprawling Stikine Icefield, which feeds those three, as well as dozens of smaller mountain glaciers. This is a near-vertical landscape of ice, water and stone, where vegetation struggles for footholds and sheer cliffs of 500 to 1,000 feet are commonplace. Yet, due to coastal mists and steady year-round precipitation (this is, after all, a temperate rainforest), bands of verdant greenery add contrast to the dominating starkness. Due to the rugged nature of the terrain, the only practical way to explore the area is via the deep, saltwater passages carved into this wilderness by the hands of ice. And, while the much larger Endicott and its smaller offshoot, Fords Terror, have their own beauty (the latter, as its dramatic name suggests, is guarded at a narrow passage by roiling tidal currents), Tracy Arm is without question the crown jewel of the three fjords. As such, it receives far and away the most visitors—a number that seems destined to grow each year.

ABOVE: Aerial view of South Sawyer Glacier and Sawyer Island.

TRACY ARM — FORDS TERROR WILDERNESS

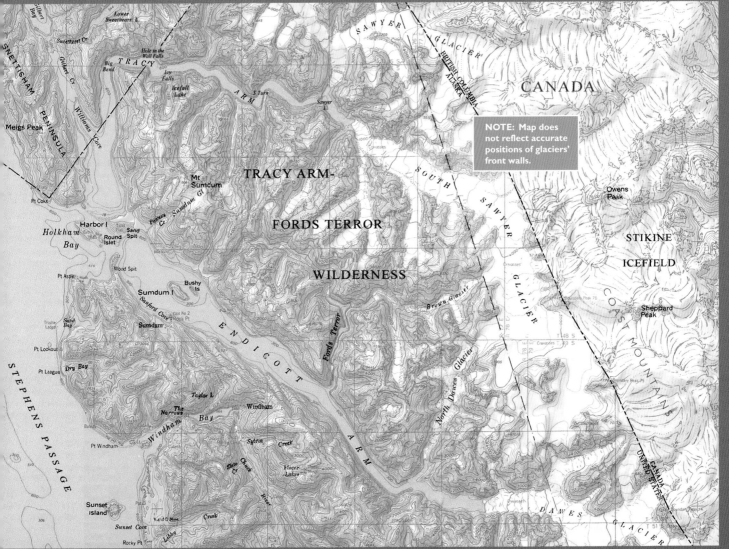

Gilbert Bay
Lower Sweetheart L.
Sweetheart Cr.
SNETTISHAM PENINSULA
Gilbert Cr.
Big Bend
TRACY
Hole in the Wall Falls
Icy Falls
Icefall Lake
ARM
S Turn
SAWYER
GLACIER
BRITISH COLUMBIA
ALASKA
CANADA
Williams Cove
Meigs Peak
Sawyer I.
Pt Coke
Mt Sumdum
Powers Cr.
Sumdum Gl.
TRACY ARM-
FORDS TERROR
WILDERNESS
Crevasses
SOUTH
SAWYER
GLACIER

NOTE: Map does not reflect accurate positions of glaciers' front walls.

Owens Peak
STIKINE
ICEFIELD
Harbor I.
Holkham Bay
Round Islet
Sand Spit
Wood Spit
Pt Astley
Sumdum I.
Bushy Is
Sanford Cove
Clot No 2
Rock Pt
Sumdum
Crevasses
Brown Glacier
GLACIER
COAST MOUNTAINS
Sheppard Peak
Sand Bay
Triable Ledge
Pt Lockout
Dry Bay
Pt League
ENDICOTT
Fords Terror
North Dawes Glacier
CANADA
UNITED STATES
STEPHENS PASSAGE
Taylor L.
The Narrows
Windham
Bay
Windham
Sylvia
Creek
ARM
Pt Windham
State Chuck Cr.
Mineer Lakes
River
DAWES
Sunset Island
Sunset Cove
Creek
Rocky Pt
Libby
GLACIER

Baseline topographic map courtesy USGS

Visitors on the *Adventure Bound* survey the ice-choked water in front of Sawyer Glacier.

The first human inhabitants of the area — the Tlingit Indians and their ancestors — left few signs of their presence inside Tracy Arm proper, where the near-vertical landscape discouraged settlements. No doubt the abundance of seals attracted hunters, however. Muir noted a Tlingit fort on Round Island at the mouth of Holkham Bay and a village at Powers Creek in Endicott Arm. However, these settlements were abandoned in the 1900s. Gold miners came and went, as well as fox farmers who used the islands in Holkham and Endicott Arm as pens. But these, too, dwindled. Today, there are no permanent residents inside Holkham Bay proper — though U.S. Forest Service rangers patrol the area by kayak six months a year, monitoring resource use and assisting researchers. And, of course, there is the increasing flood of visitors. Arguably the single person most familiar with Tracy Arm is tour boat operator Steve Weber, captain of the *Adventure Bound*. He's made an astounding 1,550 trips over 12 seasons. "It's marvelous every day," he says. "Constantly changing. You don't get into a routine, ever. You just take the day as it comes, and it's always rewarding."

RIGHT: Enormous iceberg at the mouth of Holkham Bay drifts miles from its glacial source up Tracy Arm.

A monument to the power of ice

Tracy Arm is, above all, a monument to the power of ice. The landscape was carved by its unimaginable force, a dynamic process that continues to this day. Picture a solid block of stone (predominately erosion-resistant gneiss [granite], marble and schist, with deposits of softer slate, green schist and limestone) 35 miles long and 5 wide — billions of cubic tons, up-thrust into jagged, soaring peaks. This was the raw material from which this fjord and its setting were cut by a wall of ice more than a mile thick, and by the grinding power of the rock it moved. During the height of the Pleistocene Age, the current glacial epoch, this ice monster shifted relentlessly across the land. It lumbered seaward, pulled by the force of gravity, gouging and shaping as it went, the weight so immense that it bowed the underlying bedrock. When it met the ocean, its front face, undercut as it was shoved forward, calved in immense blue shards.

TIP OF THE ICEBERG
About 90 percent of an iceberg remains below the surface of the water. Glacier ice is less dense than the surrounding seawater, and therefore floats with its bulk largely hidden. This explains the expression, "tip of the iceberg."

The vessel *Spirit of Columbia* is dwarfed by the grandeur of Sawyer Glacier.

A 32-foot Nordic Tug passes by the glacier-carved vertical walls of Tracy Arm.

...walls more than 8,000 feet high

So much of the world's water was tied up in ice that the ocean's level was far lower than it is today. The floor of Tracy Arm, at its deepest spot more than 1,200 feet below sea level, was once the bottom of a U-shaped valley with walls more than 8,000 feet high. Only the tips of the tallest surrounding peaks, known as nunataks, escaped the glacial scouring. Here a few plants and animals found refuge from the pouring river of ice, and some survived to later repopulate the land as the flood receded. Today these nunataks are visible as ragged sentinels, rising over domes that, like the walls below them, bear the horizontal striations of their sculptor's massive hand.

At its peak, the ice wall extended to the mouth of Holkham Bay, the entry point to the Tracy Arm-Fords Terror Wilderness. Here lies a terminal moraine — a huge, oblong mound of rocky rubble — that today forms a reef through which the relentless tides have carved a narrow passage into Tracy Arm.

RIGHT: Horizontal striations, evidence of the glacier's advance and retreat, scar the rock walls.

...clogged with drifting, grinding ice

Since roughly 10,000 years ago, the Stikine Icefield, like most others in Alaska and worldwide, has been generally receding — though with numerous surges forward. The most recent began in the 12th century and ended just over 100 years ago. The ice front has been in constant flux. In 1794, a party from British explorer George Vancouver's expedition briefly entered Holkham Bay and reported "much floating ice," but little else. We can't say where the glacial front lay, aside from the obvious fact it was farther in. A century later, John Muir bore due north from the mouth of Holkham and entered Tracy Arm itself. His report includes only one glacier, suggesting that Sawyer and South Sawyer glaciers, currently separated by about three water miles, were connected at the time, much farther down the fjord. Since then, the retreat shows no sign of abating.

The 120-person catamaran glides by the South Sawyer Glacier face.

Though both Sawyers continue to flow downhill, the rate of calving and melting exceeds their advance. Currently, the more active of the two is South Sawyer, which, in 2004, calved so profusely that the entire upper Arm was sometimes clogged with drifting, grinding ice — as it "galloped" (in glacial terms) backward a half-mile. Whether that trend continues remains uncertain; but if present conditions continue, the retreat of ice seems inevitable. The recession is so rapid that current maps and charts don't reflect the position of either glacier's front wall.

LEFT: Icebergs calved off the face of South Sawyer Glacier range in color from pure white to deep blue.

RETREAT / RECEDING

Despite a constant flow downhill, the Sawyer, South Sawyer and Dawes glaciers are all receding. These glaciers are losing ice faster than they can transport it. Over the eons, glaciers have advanced and retreated (receded) according to the cycles of climatic warming and cooling. The current trend of global warming has most of the world's glaciers retreating.

Until 2004, the three glaciers in Tracy Arm-Fords Terror Wilderness were in a stable, somewhat predictable retreat. But in the summer of 2004, the 20-mile long South Sawyer Glacier started galloping backwards and lost over a half-mile of ice from its terminus in Tracy Arm.

LEFT: Iceberg soup chokes the passageway to the South Sawyer Glacier.

The only constant is change.

The journey up the Arm is more than a 32-mile voyage; it's a passage back into time, to a world our Pleistocene ancestors must have known intimately. In a matter of miles, we pass through centuries of change, traced by the succession of vegetation patterns. Near the Arm's mouth, the world is comparatively soft and green, with broad patches of spruce and western hemlock. As we travel inland 10 miles, past the "big bend" — a dramatic 90-degree turn in the fjord's course from north to east — these evergreens diminish in frequency and size and gradually give way to pioneering bands of birch, willow and alder. In other places, early anchoring species such as lichens, fireweed and sedges cling to toeholds in the rock. As we near the Arm's head, barren, striated granite walls

A private boat approaches the Hole in the Wall Waterfall.

predominate, and we end our journey at shifting walls of ice: Sawyer and South Sawyer glaciers. Each is bordered by newly exposed rock, that lay under a cold, shifting mantle of ice for untold centuries. In this succession, there are no precise demarcations; the shifts are more patchwork than regular, based on local conditions including exposure, steepness and available soil. Given time, the power of growing roots, running water, and the cycle of freezing and thawing will eventually break down even dominant granite into soil, and the earth will blaze green. Or perhaps the tide of ice will turn and the glaciers will surge anew over the land, erasing all in their path as they have before. The only constant in Tracy Arm is change.

The *Wilderness Adventurer* noses her bow under the Hole in the Wall Waterfall for a crew member's shower.

Cruise ship passengers enjoy a side trip in an inflatable.

The pure spectacle of ice

Given the origins of Tracy Arm, it's only fitting that so many travelers are lured by the pure spectacle of ice. The dramatic, crevasse-riddled faces of Sawyer Glacier and that of its larger sister, South Sawyer, reign over the upper Arm, mysterious and ever-changing, sometimes shearing off in thunderous displays. Sawyer is roughly a quarter-mile across and eight miles long; South Sawyer is three times longer and half again as wide. Both average 200 feet in height where they meet tidewater, though the ice face continues far below the waterline — 300 additional feet at Sawyer, and an incredible 900 feet at its larger sister.

ICEBERGS AND GLACIERS

Glaciers form on land as a result of the net accumulation of snow over hundreds, if not thousands of years. Successive layers compress earlier layers until, at depths below roughly 200 feet, glacier ice is formed. Glaciers flow outward under their own weight like a viscous fluid. When the edge of a glacier advances into the water, the ice chunks that crumble off (calve) are called icebergs.

The largest icebergs usually calve underwater. The ice face of South Sawyer Glacier rises 200 feet above sea level and is approximately 900 feet deep below sea level. Most boat captains try to keep a minimum of a quarter-mile distance from the face of the glacier. They are not worried about the calving ice falling on the boat, but of the underwater calving that causes the largest icebergs to shoot out and up unpredictably. These potentially dangerous bergs are thus called shooters.

A boat passenger closely inspects a deep blue iceberg.

Growlers and burgy-bits

A notable fact of both Sawyer glaciers is the relative abundance of deep-blue ice — formed under greater pressure and generally older than the lighter shades. This blue color also contributes to the spectacular array of free-floating ice of all sizes — from massive icebergs to low-lying "growlers" to the minor chunks dubbed "bergy bits." Carved by the effects of sun and water, some resemble abstract sculpture as they jostle on the tide, gradually fading away. The greatest concentration of ice is near the glacial faces, especially South Sawyer. Larger bergs survive long enough to reach the open waters of Stephens Passage, beyond Holkham Bay.

BLUE ICE

Glacier blue ice provides one of nature's most vivid color displays. Snowflakes or snow crystals become glacier ice when compressed under the weight of continuous snowfalls over many years. The massive weight of the ice pushes out the tiny air pockets between the crystals, producing an extremely dense, clear, air-free ice. As light strikes this ice, its crystalline structure absorbs all the colors of the light spectrum except blue. The blue light is reflected off the ice, giving the ice the intense blue color that we see.

When ice calves off a glacier, the newly exposed ice appears exceptionally blue. The crystalline ice structure responsible for the blue color remains intact for only a few days. In time, air and surface melt breaks down the ice, causing it to fade to white — a color that denotes many tiny air bubbles in the ice.

Deep-blue ice contrasts with the faded blue to white icebergs floating in front of the face of South Sawyer.

Wildlife in Tracy Arm

Of course, wildlife is a highlight of any visit to the Arm. Seeing harbor seals is a virtual lock — dozens, sometimes hundreds, are visible on the ice floes near South Sawyer, which serve both as havens from shore predators (especially for young pups, who are born on the ice in late spring) and as sunning platforms, where the animals warm themselves and rest. Mountain goats, too, are regularly spied by sharp-eyed viewers, often hundreds or thousands of feet up the Arm's sheer rock walls. During early season, April and sometimes May, goats may browse just above sea level, searching for the first tender shoots or even foraging for seaweed. Black bears are present throughout Tracy Arm, patrolling the intertidal zone, especially early and late in the day. Sea birds — including arctic terns, marbled murrelets and pigeon guillemots (easily identified by their red feet) — are common near the glaciers. Larger marine mammals, such as humpback whales, killer whales, Steller sea lions and harbor porpoises, are rare inside the Arm proper, but are commonly spied on the 45-mile journey between Stephens Passage and Juneau.

Harbor seals by the dozens haul out and rest on the icebergs.

Harbor seals

More than a 1,000 harbor seals use the icebergs close to the glacier fronts as haul-outs during the summer in Tracy Arm-Fords Terror Wilderness. The icebergs afford the seals protection from land predators such as wolves and their only marine predators, the killer whales. The most concentrated use of the ice is in front of the South Sawyer Glacier. Usually the harbor seals move onto the icebergs in the spring in order to have their babies (pups).

Harbor seals are, of course, mammals; that is, they are hairy, warm-blooded, air-breathing animals that suckle their young. Pups weigh about 24 pounds at birth and adults weight in around 180 pounds with males slightly larger than females.

Harbor seals can dive to depths exceeding 600 feet and can remain submerged for more than 20 minutes. Female average life expectancy is 32 years, while a typical male lives 26 years.

Harbor seals are frequently seen breaking the surface of the water to cast an inquisitive eye.

Black bears

Black bears are most visible in Tracy Arm during the early summer months of May and June. Just re-entering the world after a winter's hibernation, the bears forage along the tide line. Later in the season the bears leave the shoreline and move back up the river valleys (out of sight) to feed on plants and berries.

Black bears are the smallest of the North American bears. Adult bears stand about 30 inches at the shoulders and measure about 60 inches from nose to tail. Males outsize females, and an average adult weighs about 180 to 200 pounds.

A black bear eats spring grasses and sedges.

Mountain goats

Mountain goats thrive along Tracy Arm's steep rocky slopes. This vertical environment provides unparalleled protection for the goats from their predators. In the summer the goats move into high alpine meadows 2,000 to 5,000 feet above the Arm's shoreline. During the winter goats move out of the high country, seeking escape from the deep snow. In the spring, visitors to the Arm can sometimes find goats at tide line.

Goats live for approximately 10 to 12 years. Males (billies) weigh in around 200 pounds and females (nannies) at around 160. Nannies usually give birth to a single baby (kid) in late May or early June. At birth the kids weigh approximately seven pounds and stand a foot high at the shoulders. Kids are precocious and can keep up with adults on the steep rocky terrain when only hours old.

A mountain goat kid smells its mother or nanny.

A group of mountain goats forage in the seaweed at low tide just off the face of Sawyer Glacier.

Bald eagle in spruce tree.

Bald eagles

The white heads of bald eagles dot the spruce trees along the route to Tracy Arm. Often, the eagles will perch on icebergs in the Arm. Southeast Alaska's bald eagle population by itself is larger than in all the other states combined.

The United States' national symbol remains brown until sexual maturity between 4 and 6 years old when the eagle's head and tail feathers turn distinctively white. Bald eagles can live up to 30 years, but the average life spans 15 to 20 years. They grow about three feet tall, weigh 10 to 15 pounds, and have a six-foot plus wing span.

Arctic terns

The arctic tern holds the record for the longest migration of any bird. Their approximate 21,000-mile round-trip migration takes them from Antarctica to Alaska. These lightweight birds (10 to 12 ounces) spend their summer in Tracy Arm, living around the edges at the face of the glaciers. These all-white birds have a distinctive black skull cap, red legs and a long, white, forked, swallow-like tail. They eat small fish, insects, krill and shrimp and live up to 20 years.

Arctic tern on iceberg.

The humpback whale's name comes from the distinctive rounded hump around its dorsal fin, visible just before it dives.

Humpback whales

The passage from Juneau to Tracy Arm can provide a good opportunity to see humpback whales. Humpbacks and killer whales typically do not enter Tracy Arm proper. The humpback whales usually congregate outside Holkham Bay in Stephens Passage, often in great numbers in August and September.

Humpbacks grow to lengths of 42 to 49 feet and weigh 25 to 40 tons with females being larger than males. Humpbacks are the sixth largest whale species in the world.

Humpbacks belong to a sub-order of whales called baleen or toothless whales. Their throats are no wider than a grapefruit, and they savor dense clouds of

Accompanied by two other whales, a humpback raises its tail before sounding.

zooplankton (mostly comprised of a shrimp-like crustacean called krill), and schools of herring-sized fish. They feed by taking a mouthful of prey-laden seawater, straining out the water, and gulping down what is left. The straining apparatus, known as baleen, hangs from the upper jaws in place of teeth and resembles rows of fine-toothed combs.

Humpbacks migrate, wintering in Hawaii or Mexico (where they give birth) and summering in Alaska, where the cold water combines with the long summer daylight to produce a sea rich in prey. Humpback feed almost constantly and consume over a third of a ton of food per day.

Supporting a six-foot tall dorsal fin, a large male killer whale cruises the inland waters of Southeast Alaska.

Killer whales

Killer whales are the wolves of the marine world. They usually hunt in packs, are the apex predators of the ocean, and cover a huge territory, sometimes thousands of square miles as their home range. A passenger is as likely to see a killer whale along the route to Tracy Arm as anywhere else in Southeast Alaska.

These toothed whales typically travel in family groups called pods. Killer whales average 23 to 33 feet and weigh 4 to 8 tons, depending on the sex of the animal, the males are larger. Familiar as the whale species featured at Sea World, the killer whales' distinctive black and white markings make them easily recognizable in the wild. As track stars of the ocean world, these whales can reach speeds of approximately 34 miles per hour. Ancient whalers referred to them as "killers of whales" for their ability to kill much larger whales. Over time the name shortened to killer whale. Many people, in the interest of a kinder, gentler image, call them orcas.

RIGHT: A killer whale surfaces while another lurks just below the water along the shoreline of Southeast Alaska.

Icy Falls, Tracy Arm.

A brush against the eternal

In the end, a journey to Tracy Arm isn't about a checklist of creatures spotted, a collection of facts or figures, or an accounting of miles on a map. Surely such details add richness, but ultimate meaning lies in grasping the magnitude of what you've seen — the drama of creation and destruction that lies at the heart of all being, cast in a scale so grand it must be felt rather than understood. And fleeting images fill in the rest — skeins of mist draped across mountain shoulders, the sudden appearance of a seal's long-whiskered face at boatside, angled sunlight filtering through an iceberg. These are the small things that fuse into memory, reminding us we've brushed against the eternal.

From Juneau to Tracy Arm

ALASKA

Map Area

N
W — E
S

8 miles
0 2 4 6 8

Taku River

Whiting River

Speel River

TAKU INLET

★ Juneau

Slocum Inlet

Taku Harbor

Limestone Harbor

Port Snettisham

Lucky Me

Marmion Is

Grand Is

Douglas Island

Admiralty Island

STEPHENS